"YOU ARE PERFECT

JUST THE WAY YOU ARE"

ETTA ROSE

Published by LuLu Taylor

ISBN: 978-0-473-57263-1

All rights reserved. No part of this publication may be reproduced, stored in a retrieval system or transmitted by any form in any means, electronic, mechanical, photocopying, recording or otherwise, without prior written permission of the publisher and copyright holders.
The moral right of the author has been asserted.

Text copyright © LuLu Taylor 2021
Illustration copyright © Bec Brown 2021

Printed by Ingram Spark Australia 2021

ETTA ROSE

THIS BOOK IS DEDICATED TO MY BEAUTIFUL FAMILY.
THANK YOU FOR GIVING ME THE GIFT OF KNOWING
HOW IT FEELS TO BE UNCONDITIONALLY LOVED,
AND FOR BELIEVING IN ME IN THE TIMES WHEN I
HAD STOPPED BELIEVING IN MYSELF.

ETTA ROSE LOVES LOVELY CLOTHES,
BUT SHE DOESN'T LIKE PINK
AND SHE DOESN'T LIKE BOWS

HER OTHER FRIENDS DO, AND THAT'S OK,
ETTA STILL LOVES TO DRESS HER OWN WAY!

SOMETIMES PEOPLE STARE AT HER LONG SPOTTY SOCKS,

BUT SHE DOESN'T CARE AND LOVES WEARING BRIGHT FROCKS

TODAY HER HAIR IS TIED UP WITH A COLOURFUL BANDANA,

AND A HAIRCLIP SHE MADE,
FROM A BROOCH FROM HER NANA

ETTA ROSE THINKS IT'S FUN WEARING
SPARKLY BLUE SHOES,

AND SAYS,
"IT'S NOBODY'S BUSINESS
WHAT COLOUR SHOES I SHOULD CHOOSE"

IF SHE FEELS LIKE WEARING PAISLEY, SHE SAYS,

"I JOLLY WELL WILL"

AND ADDS,

"I MAY EVEN WEAR IT WITH A BIG, RUFFLY, FRILL"

ETTA LIKES MAKING NEW THINGS,
FROM THINGS THAT ARE OLD,
SHE LOVES ADDING BUTTONS
AND SEQUINS OF GOLD

IF SOMETHING IS DULL, SHE MAKES IT
BRIGHTER AND BETTER!
SHE GIVES THE WORLD MORE COLOUR AND
MAKES THINGS MORE 'ETTA'!

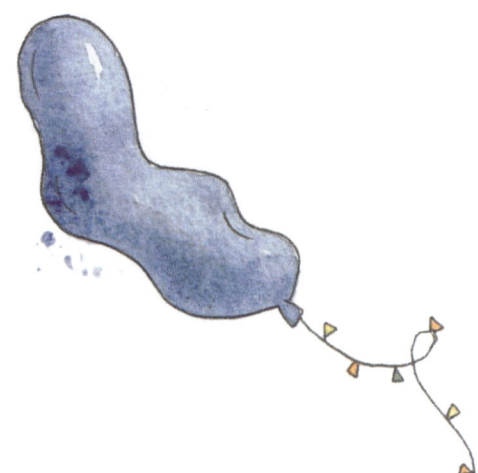

PUFFY CHECKED PANTS AND T-SHIRTS WITH FACES,
THEN ON SOME DAYS SHE LIKES TO WEAR BRACES

THEY MAKE HER FEEL FANCY,
AND THEY LOOK VERY SWEET,
AND THEY STOP HER PANTS FROM
ENDING UP AT HER FEET!

Even on days that are rainy and cold,
Etta's style is still a sight to behold

Her parka is red and flowery and fun,
and her wellies are yellow and
bright like the sun

WITH LAYERS OF BEADS AND BROOCHES ON HER CLOTHES,

 ETTA LOOKS FABULOUS, WHEREVER SHE GOES!

SHE IS ALWAYS SMILEY AND
KIND TO HER FRIENDS

SHE SAYS,
"BEING NICE IS THE MOST IMPORTANT OF TRENDS"

WHEN PEOPLE ASK ETTA FOR TIPS ON LOOKING NICE,
SHE GIVES THEM HER BESTEST PIECE OF ADVICE...

"WHAT IS MOST IMPORTANT" SAYS ETTA
"AND WHATEVER YOU DO,
YOU MUST ALWAYS REMEMBER, TO
<u>ALWAYS</u> BE YOU"

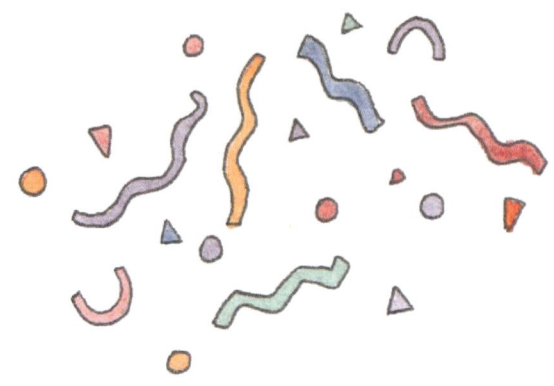

"THEN, NO MATTER THE SHOES,
NO MATTER THE CLOTHES,

AND WHETHER YOU LOVE RED,
OR SPARKLES OR BOWS…….

WHEREVER YOU ARE
AND WHATEVER YOU DO,

YOU'LL BE LOOKING YOUR BEST,
BECAUSE YOU'RE LOOKING LIKE

YOU!"

MEET THE CREATORS OF ETTA ROSE

LULU TAYLOR has a love of rhyming, singing loudly by herself in the car, fun, laughter and pottering around on the family lifestyle block in South Canterbury, which she shares with her husband, children and collection of eccentric pets. She is on a mission to spread the word that it's cool to be kind and to think about what we can do to make the world a better place!
You can connect with her at @picklesandstitches

BEC BROWN lives with her beautiful son, by the beach in New Zealand.
If she isn't in her garden art studio, you'll find her paddle boarding, playing at the beach, or hunting the local op-shops for treasures!
"It was an absolute treat to illustrate this book for Lu"
"No one is you - and that is your superpower!"
You can connect with her at @cloudsofcolour

Printed in the USA
CPSIA information can be obtained
at www.ICGtesting.com
LVRC092327081123
763461LV00030B/130